WHAT DO YOU SAY TO A BURNING BUSH?

Sermons For
Pentecost (Middle Third)
Cycle A, First Lesson Texts

STEVE BURT

CSS Publishing Company, Inc.
Lima, Ohio

WHAT DO YOU SAY TO A BURNING BUSH?

Scripture quotations are from the *New Revised Standard Version of the Bible,* copyright 1989, by the Division of Christian Education of the National Council of the Churches of Christ in the USA. Used by permission.

Library of Congress Cataloging-in-Publication Data

Burt, Steven E., 1949-
    What do you say to a burning bush? : sermons for Pentecost (middle third) : cycle A, first lesson texts / Steven Burt
       p.   cm.
    ISBN 0-78880-0457-3
    1. Bible. O.T. Genesis—Sermons. 2. Pentecost season—Sermons. 3. Sermons, American. I. Title.
BS1235.4.B87   1995
252'.6—dc20   95-12290
                                             CIP

This book is available in the following formats, listed by ISBN:
0-7880-0457-3 Book
0-7880-0458-1 IBM 3 1/2 computer disk
0-7880-0459-X IBM 3 1/2 book and disk package
0-7880-0460-3 Macintosh computer disk
0-7880-0461-1 Macintosh book and disk package
0-7880-0462-X IBM 5 1/4 computer disk
0-7880-0463-8 IBM 5 1/4 book and disk package

This book is dedicated to my wife Jo Ann and my patient and kind congregation, the United Church of Stonington, Connecticut. Jo Ann read and critiqued draft after draft, keeping me humble. Through the summer of 1994 the congregation sat through my preaching of what were essentially second drafts of these sermons. Their helpful feedback moved me along to third, fourth, and final drafts. Those same folks also challenged me to find good illustrations. For Jo Ann's and my congregation's help I am deeply grateful.

Table Of Contents

Proper 12
Pentecost 10
Ordinary Time 17
Genesis 29:15-28

What Do You Do When Life Ain't Fair?

Life doesn't always hand us what we want when we want it. In those times there's the temptation to shortcut, or to do the unethical, or to run from the problem. It's then that we need to keep our eyes on our goals and keep plugging along, honestly and diligently.

A farmer's crops failed one year because of the drought. The previous year there had been too much rain, and it had flooded everything. The year before that he'd suffered due to an influx of imports. Discouraged, the farmer went fishing far off the beaten path along a wilderness stream. He caught a few trout, then lay on the bank to enjoy the sandwiches he had brought for lunch.

A beaver appeared, dragging a branch. It chose a spot where the stream split off into a little rivulet, then placed the branch where the water rippled over rocks like a washboard. The fisherman could see the beaver was seeking to dam that smaller stream to form a quieter pond.

The beaver disappeared, returning with another branch which it put next to the first. A while later, another. But while the beaver was gone, the three branches washed away, carried off downstream by the current.

"Bad place to build, Mr. Beaver," the farmer said.

But the beaver returned and put a new branch in the spot, then a second, a third, a fourth. The fisherman was nervous for the beaver, knowing it could wash out any time.

A brown bear appeared, swatting trout near the fledgling dam. One fish eluded it, and when the bear clumsily swung its paw again, there went the four branches of the dam floating downstream. The farmer shook his head. "Fate is against you, Mr. Beaver," he said. The bear left.

The beaver reappeared, placed a fresh branch where the first and subsequent ones had been. More branches followed.

The farmer couldn't believe the beaver refused to give up, so he waded into the stream and dislodged the branches, which floated downstream. He returned to the bank.

The beaver showed up, dragged a new branch into place, then another and another until finally the dam was secure and could withstand the water pressure. The moving stream became a quiet pool of backwaters. The farmer took his fishing rod and went home to decide if he would farm again.

Sometimes it feels as if things are going against us. The forces of nature. An accident. Illness or injury. Or other people participate in our undoing — sometimes without even knowing it, but at other times with malicious intent. Many forces work to set us back or keep us from our goals. It can be depressing and discouraging, and at times it can make us feel like giving up. Or we may be tempted to employ deceit or shortcuts.

It's at those times we must keep our sights on the goal, acting honestly and diligently, no matter what others are doing around us.

Today's scripture passage reflects conditions as they were 3,000 years ago. Let's flatly note that attitudes and treatment of women were very different than today. That said, let's not get hung up on those issues here. Instead let's look at what the scripture writers are lifting up to us as the key story thread here: Jacob's winning of his true love despite the many adversities placed in his path.

Jacob is advised by his father to seek out great-uncle Laban in a nearby land, which he does. So Jacob becomes a foreigner in Uncle Laban's country. As a foreigner, he hasn't got the rights a citizen might have had. He knows little of the rules, regulations, social customs and mores.

No sooner does he arrive than he glimpses his distant cousin Rachel who has probably not yet reached puberty. It's love at first sight.

Keep in mind that we know something of Jacob's background and his behavior patterns. In one incident he managed to get his very hungry, slower-witted, elder brother Esau to hand over his rights as firstborn son in exchange for a bowl of soup (Genesis 25:29-34). In another incident Jacob slips into his nearly-blind old father's tent and pretends to be Esau, in the process tricking their father into conferring the patriarch's blessing on him (Jacob) instead of on Esau (Genesis 27:18-27). So the Jacob we see in his growing-up years is deceptive, shrewd, a master of manipulation. Now, however, he is a stranger in a foreign land.

Uncle Laban has another daughter besides Rachel. Rachel is actually the younger of the two; Leah is the elder. They are close in age and look very much alike except that the elder Leah has very different eyes, perhaps a paler color or something else unique that is more obvious in daylight.

But Jacob loves the younger Rachel. He asks Uncle Laban if he can have her hand when she achieves marriageable age. Uncle Laban says okay, but what is to be the dowry? (Jacob, you see, is broke. He hasn't had time to build up his own herd of sheep or goats yet, so he hasn't anything to offer.) Jacob, absolutely smitten with Rachel, says, "How about if I work tending your flocks for seven years, Uncle Laban?" Even by the standards of that day, Jacob's offer went far beyond generous. He might have gotten Laban to accept four or five years of service. But Jacob, being a newcomer to the country, is probably ignorant of what an adequate dowry might be (and he's madly in love), so he rushes in with an offer of seven years of service. Uncle Laban quickly says okay.

A couple of roadblocks so far. First, Jacob is a foreigner and lacks the rights of a citizen. Tied to that is his lack of knowledge of customs, which would have helped him negotiate the dowry more fairly. (He's like a gullible tourist at an Acapulco open-air marketplace. He doesn't know everything is negotiable and dickering is expected.) The big block, though, is that he's now got to work and wait seven years for Rachel.

Finally, the time arrives for nuptials week. Uncle Laban brings his daughter to Jacob's tent for the night. Now remember, the two sisters Leah and Rachel look very much alike except for their eyes. No doubt the daughter whom Uncle Laban has brought to Jacob's tent has her veil on. It is dark outside and dark in the tent. Jacob has probably tipped a few bottles of wine at the evening's nuptial festivities. To that we add the intrigue factor — Uncle Laban's deception!

Morning arrives, Jacob awakens, and whom does he find lying beside him? Leah, the elder sister! Seven years of honest work when he might have contracted for less, and still Jacob doesn't get his true love Rachel.

Confronted with his deceit, Laban offers a lame excuse. "Around this neck of the woods," he says, "we don't allow the younger sister to be married off before the elder sister." Laban is trying to snare Jacob in a you-didn't-know-the-custom trap. But the question remains about Laban's integrity: Why didn't he spell that out before, seven years earlier?

Uncle Laban has deceived his nephew, and it must be tempting for Jacob to consider deceiving Uncle Laban in return, paying back evil with evil (something Jesus would admonish us centuries later not to do). At the very least, Jacob must be considering eloping, asking Rachel to flee the country with him.

But he does neither. Despite his personal history of deceit and manipulation, Jacob stays the true course. He says, "Uncle Laban, how can I gain your *legitimate* permission to wed your daughter Rachel?" He'll do it the right way even though he's been wronged.

Laban tells him he can have Rachel in marriage within a week — if he'll agree to stay around after the wedding and do another seven years as herd foreman! Another seven years. It seems pretty unfair — he's already done the agreed-upon seven years — but at least Jacob can marry his beloved Rachel with her father's blessing. Jacob agrees to the terms. (Eventually, with the help of surrogate mothers, he fathers eleven children, one of whom is Joseph, the lad to whom he will give the famed coat of many colors.)

For all his manipulation and deceit earlier in life, Jacob has kept his eyes on the prize, his true love Rachel. He has done it with diligence and honesty even when everything seemed to be working against him. He faced the fact that life doesn't always give you what you want when you want it. Jacob was like that beaver. He kept at it, branch by branch by branch.

In Burlington, Vermont, there's an organization called Vermont Cares, a non-profit volunteer network created to help people with HIV/AIDS and their families and friends to get the physical, financial and emotional support they need. But there have been difficulties since its beginnings — funding difficulties, prejudice, hatemongers and fearmongers stirring up the community against it, acts of vandalism. What appeared at first to be its death knell came in the spring of 1994 when an arsonist torched the building which housed the organization. The fire destroyed the building and practically everything in it, including the contents of the Vermont Cares offices: files, records, mailing lists of clients, contributors, volunteers, mementoes, pictures and histories which recorded the struggles of victims and their loved ones. It felt as if the dam had let go.

But what wasn't washed away was the spirit, the tenacity, the integrity, the vision of the goal.

A 23-year-old volunteer named Wendy believed in the mission of Vermont Cares. She had been working as a restaurant hostess since finishing college, and only six months earlier had helped organize a free holiday dinner for the city's hungry and lonely at Thanksgiving. To feed those 400 people Wendy had had to learn to solicit donations, develop a plan of action, and recruit, train and coordinate 75 volunteers.

Her idea for raising Vermont Cares from the ashes was to put on an auction outside City Hall. So she applied her newly-developed planning and promotion skills to the task of soliciting donations and recruiting volunteers from around the city. Plenty of roadblocks appeared: reluctance of some merchants to donate, bureaucratic snags with the required permits, telephone volunteers not showing up at the appointed times. But this young woman kept her eyes on the goal and moved ahead a branch at a time, building, building, building.

The day of the auction arrived and the auctioneer didn't show. Half the tents didn't arrive, and rain clouds threatened on the horizon. The sound system developed problems. But bidders showed up and huddled under what tents were available. Wendy's boyfriend Damon, a part-time disk jockey for weddings and parties, filled in as auctioneer. The hope was to raise $1,000. When the day's receipts were in, Vermont Cares had $4,000 to rise from the ashes.

We, too, are called to be like that young woman Wendy — honest, hardworking, diligent — as individuals and as congregations. This is real life, and we can count on trials and tribulations. There are bound to be setbacks, roadblocks, natural disasters, even personal betrayals that threaten to thwart our progress toward our goal. As with the beaver building the dam, the force of the water itself will at times wash away our work; the bear will smash it to smithereens; the mischievous fisherman will dismantle it.

But like the beaver building the dam, like Jacob pursuing Rachel, like Vermont Cares serving AIDS victims and their loved ones, we too, with God's help, will achieve our goals. We must remain faithful, keep our eyes on the prize, and be honest and diligent. May God add a blessing to our work.

The Face Of God

Here we're dealing with the story of Jacob at the Jabbok River Crossing, an incident in which he wrestles all night and secures a blessing. It's a strange incident, isn't it? We've got something which occurred a thousand or more years before Jesus' time, something reminiscent of superstitions and primitive religions: a man wrestling for a blessing with a creature that must escape before the light of day, like a vampire or a werewolf. This is a strange portion of the Bible to have to deal with.

Maybe it would help to know something of the background of this fellow Jacob. He's an up-and-comer, a go-getter, an aggressive and shrewd climber. And he doesn't always play his cards "according to Hoyle." He uses his wits and his strength to claw his way up in the world.

In other passages about Jacob and his brother, we see that they are the children of Isaac. Esau is the elder of the two, and the birthright should rightfully be his. But the younger Jacob gets Esau, at a time when Esau is starving, to sign over his rights as firstborn son in exchange for a bowl of lentil soup. Pretty shrewd.

13

In another incident we see something similar happening, not with the birthright, but with the father's blessing. In this other story father Isaac is near death and can barely see any longer. He wants to discharge his fatherly blessing, something very important and powerful. By rights it should go to the elder son Esau. But Jacob sneaks into his father's tent dressed in Esau's clothes. He disguises his voice so it sounds like his brother's, takes advantage of his father's failing eyesight, and steals the blessing meant for Esau.

Then, rather than risk his brother Esau's wrath, Jacob clears out of town and settles in another country. As luck would have it (or maybe there's no luck about it, knowing Jacob), he marries well. Eventually he makes a fortune in business. When we encounter him here, Jacob is, by the world's standards, very successful. He learned early on how to manipulate situations to make things happen.

Jacob is at the Jabbok River Crossing. Imagine it. Jacob is sitting at his campfire, staring into the flames. His ears pick up a sound in the underbrush behind him, the sound of a dry twig snapping underfoot. Expecting no one, Jacob whirls and — whump! — his attacker's body hits him full force, knocking him to the ground. The two of them, Jacob and his unknown attacker, grapple and roll and twist. Jacob cannot see the face of his attacker. It is too dark and too confused. The man is strong, stronger than anyone he has ever encountered, perhaps stronger than any human being.

They continue the struggle all night, their grunts and heavy breathing and the crunch of snapping underbrush the only sounds to break the silence. Despite the opponent's superior strength, as the dawn begins to threaten, it is clear that, wonder of wonders, Jacob is winning. He's winning.

And then, oddly, like a werewolf or a vampire or some other-than-human creature of the night, this stranger begs Jacob to let him out of the hammerlock so he can escape before the sun rises. But it seems Jacob isn't ready to let go of the wrestler just because he's yelled "Uncle!"

That's when it happens. The wrestler simply touches Jacob on his leg, on the thigh (maybe in the place he himself had placed his own hand on Isaac's thigh to receive the father's blessing), and in an instant Jacob is, for all practical purposes, disabled. He lies helpless, crippled.

It appears that this was a charade, a cheat, a set-up. It seems that the stranger may have had the power to defeat Jacob at any time during the night, but he chose not to, at least not until morning. And then he did it with relative ease, as if he were some cross between a Kung Fu artist and an acupressurist. Maybe the unknown wrestler did it so that Jacob would realize that, though he'd almost won, all his cleverness, his strength, his desire to win wouldn't be enough. Maybe he did it to show Jacob what true defeat was.

Whatever the case, Jacob refuses to let go, his grip now like that of a person who has fallen over the edge of a cliff and is holding fast to a scraggly root. He's hanging on for dear life. At last, as the dawn begins to break, Jacob can begin to see the wrestler's face.

I like the way Fred Buechner describes what Jacob sees.

". . . something more terrible than the face of death — the face of love . . . half ruined with suffering and fierce with joy, the face a man flees down all the darkness of his days until at last he cries out, 'I will not let you go, unless you bless me!' "[1]

This is a blessing he cannot gain by shrewdness or by deception as he gained his brother's birthright and his father's deathbed blessing. Nor can he gain it by strength or by force, because this time he literally hasn't got a leg to stand on. He's in no position to finesse it or to grab it. It's clear that this stranger, this wrestler from the night who has disabled him, can just as easily disable the rest of Jacob's body. He doesn't owe Jacob a blessing. This is a blessing Jacob can only get as a gift.

The picture brings to mind a ten-year-old who sometimes wrestled on the lawn with his older and much larger cousin. After a long stretch of wrestling, the youngster always ended up on the grass, curled up and clutching the ankle of the larger cousin who was still standing. The older cousin would look down victoriously, but the younger cousin would nevertheless hang on, look up, and demand from his ridiculous position, "Okay. Give up now?" He'd continue to hang on, knowing he had lost, and ask again, "Okay. Give up?" And finally, through gales of laughter, the older and larger cousin, the victor, would say, "Yeah, yeah, I give up." And the younger one would let go his death grip on the ankle.

That's like Jacob wrestling with this angel or with God — Jacob hanging on and asking, "Okay, you gonna bless me or what?" Jacob's opponent might even have felt like laughing aloud at the utter lunacy of it all. The question of who would win the match was never in doubt. But it was only in discovering that nothing in his arsenal of weapons would work — not strength, nor cunning, nor skill — that Jacob experienced the power of unexpected mercy, the grace of God.

Look what happened as it approached first light, as the darkness dissipated and the stranger's face became visible. What did it look like, this face that stared down at a defeated Jacob clutching its ankle? What face could make Jacob gasp in shock and surprise and beg for a blessing? What could cause him to say, "Oh, God, bless me, bless me"?

Think for a moment about faces. Particular faces. Faces that leave impressions on our minds. Not just any faces. Faces that move us.

One vivid face jumps out at us from an old television commercial about litter and pollution. A Native American who looks like he stepped off an Indian Head nickel has gotten out of a canoe. He stands there, bare face twisted in pain as he views a polluted stream clogged with trash. A single tear runs down his face. It's a powerful image, a face of pain, a face that moves you.

Another is the widow's face at the funeral of a young man, her husband. He had committed suicide. She sits looking dull, stunned, in shock. Then the floodgates open, the tears start, the sobs wrack her body. The face of anguish.

Many faces imprint themselves on our consciousness. The weeping woman going through a divorce. The stoic face of the woman trying to hide the pain of a marriage and family being ripped apart by a husband's alcoholism. The glassy, wide-eyed stare of a starving African child on a Bread for the World poster. The faces all seem to project pain, loss, impending defeat, certainly not victory.

Now call to mind Jesus' face in the Garden at Gethsemane, during his dark night of the soul that is so like the Jabbok River Crossing incident when Jacob wrestles and finally submits to God's will. Jesus' face at Gethsemane is, at the least, the face of disappointment. "Couldn't you — at least you, Peter, my friend — couldn't you stay awake just one hour?"

It is a weary face, an exhausted one, with sadness and lines and crow's feet, with dark shadows and bags under the eyes. This has been a tiring, compressed ministry brimming over with conflict. Jesus' face shows it. His is a face of loneliness, for he must face not only the Gethsemane night alone, but he must face his fate — drink the bitter cup — alone. He must bear the betrayal by a friend, a betrayal with a kiss, of all things. He must bear the denial — not once, but three times — by one of his closest friends. He must face disgrace, a mock trial, scourging, crucifixion. He gets so worked up about it all, one gospel tells us, that he sweats drops of blood from his forehead. Jesus' face in the garden is the face of disappointment, loneliness, suffering.

But look. There are three other faces, too, with lips curled into sneers. Three faces of victory.

The high priest Caiaphas, who represents the religious status quo, smiles a quiet, victorious smile because this thorn in his side, this troublemaking preacher will soon be in the tomb.

King Herod, who represents the political status quo, smiles a sneering, victorious smile as well, an evil sneer, relieved that this petty threat to his kingdom, this Jesus, will soon be dead and gone.

Pontius Pilate, the Roman procurator, a petty official who doesn't want anyone riling up the insurrectionists, smiles the third smile, for this Jesus, whose actions might reflect poorly on him back in Rome, will soon be gone.

Three smiling faces of victory.

But wait! There is a fourth face of victory, too, the face of death, the skull, the awful grinning picture of the Grim Reaper. It is at times the same face we see superimposed over the face of the starving African child, or the faces of Caiaphas, Herod, Pilate. Grinning Death and sneering Victory in the same faces.

But then we see the face of Jesus, this time on the cross. He is gaunt, thin, dehydrated from hanging in the hot sun. His hair is matted; dried blood is streaked on his forehead below the crown of thorns. His eyes hollow as his face begins to take on the look of death.

But there's something different about his face. He isn't glaring in anger at the world below him. His face isn't filled with the bitterness we'd expect. Instead his eyes reflect compassion, sympathy, pity, love. It's as if he can see all the other faces from there — the Native American with the tear on his face, the starving child, the divorcing woman, the weeping widow, the wife and children of the alcoholic, the sneering, victorious Caiaphas, Herod, and Pilate.

Yes, his face is different. His spirit radiates something different, something . . . *divine.* Even there, especially there, nailed to a cross, he manages to look upon the people who have crucified him and utter the words, "Father, forgive them; they know not what they do." In this face is a strange mixture of exhaustion, suffering, sorrow, love, and forgiveness.

The Roman guard at the foot of the cross, the gospel tells us, looked into that face and was so moved he said, "Truly, this man was the Son of God."

That face the Roman guard saw is the face Jacob looked into that night at the Jabbok River Crossing as the dawn crept in on a night of wrestling and struggling. It wasn't the face Jacob expected to see after his all-night battle. It wasn't the face of victory at all, not the countenance of conquest, not someone standing over another with sneering smile and lips curled at the corners.

The face Jacob saw was the face the Roman guard saw from the foot of the cross as Jesus gasped his last and darkness covered the land. The face Jacob saw was the face Mary Magdalene saw when she looked into the darkness from outside the tomb that first Easter morning. The face Jacob saw was the face of compassion, human suffering, pain, tears, and love — above all, love. The face Jacob saw and didn't expect to see was the face of God — the loving, forgiving God who doesn't withhold blessings but gives them freely — free not for the stealing or for the outwitting, but free for the asking.

May we all see the face of Jacob's God, the face we know in Jesus Christ crucified and risen, and may we all ask for and receive the blessing.

---

1. Frederick Buechner, *The Magnificent Defeat* (New York: Seabury, 1966), p. 18.

Proper 14
Pentecost 12
Ordinary Time 19
Genesis 37:1-4, 12-28

Good Guys And Bad Guys Alike

Love your enemies, Jesus says in his Sermon on the Mount (Matthew 5). Is he serious? Crazy? Love our enemies? We ask, "Why would we do that?" And Jesus says, "So that you may be children of your Father in heaven."

Then he gets crazier. "Be perfect, therefore, as your heavenly Father is perfect." What a tall order: Be perfect!

The key to being perfect, as God is perfect, it would seem, is to understand that Jesus also says in his Sermon on the Mount that God "makes his sun rise on the evil *and* on the good, and sends rain on the righteous and on the unrighteous."

What's this? God sprinkles rain and shines sun on both the good guys and the bad guys? You mean *my* God, *your* God, *our* God, is the God of *those guys,* too? You mean God's the God of the Commies, the Iraqis, the North Vietnamese, the Muslim fundamentalists? God is the God of the *bad guys*?

Surely there must be some mistake, Jesus! Not *my* God! Not *your* God! Not *our* God! You mean God is the God of the homosexuals, the Catholics, Jerry Falwell and the fundamentalists, the Jews, the Methodists, the Republicans, the Democrats, the liberals, and the conservatives?

21

Oops! Did I mix up the bad guys and the good guys again? Sorry. You mean *my* God sprinkles rain and shines sun on Hindus, Buddhists, atheists, non-believers, those not "saved," those people who don't go to church? The bad guys? And God also sprinkles rain and shines sun on the folks who voted for George Bush? For Bill Clinton? And on the ones who voted *against* them? Whatever! The point is: God is on the other side, too. It's called *absolute grace.*

So what does Jesus mean when he tells us to be perfect like our heavenly Father? He seems to be calling for us to be perfect by loving our enemies. We are to be like God, sprinkling rain and shining sun on both sides. Jesus means we are to get on a high perch like God, then work at seeing both sides of the conflict.

The terms right, wrong, good, bad, just, and *unjust* are all used by both sides in a conflict or disagreement. Both sides insist they're good, right, justified.

If we read about the Revolutionary War, we can find books offering both the British and the American versions, from which we can see both sides were "right," "justified," "good." There were only "good guys" on both sides. The message? God alone is qualified to judge what is good.

We've just put our finger on the problem. We cannot love our enemies, sad to say, because we see them as the bad guys and ourselves as the good guys. We have a natural tendency to identify with the good guys, don't we?

We assume Judas was a bad guy, an impression the New Testament writers contribute to. They paint him as bad, having the devil enter into old Judas. That, unfortunately, tended to make Judas unavailable to us for sympathy, understanding. It's almost impossible for us to identify with him.

Is someone a bad guy because he opposes European domination over a country — as Judas opposed Roman domination over the land he loved? As our patriot fathers and mothers opposed the domination of England over us? Can't we understand a patriot like Judas, a man who would finally lose faith in his teacher when the going got tough, when this Rabbi, this Master said, "Render unto Caesar what is Caesar's"? Can't we identify with him?

And was Judas a bad guy to heed the advice of his church leaders when they advised that Jesus, this seeming pretender to the messianic throne, was roiling the waters so that the Roman legions would come crashing in too early, thereby destroying any hope of a successful rebellion? Was Judas a bad guy for accepting an honorary amount, a token, for service to his church?

But look at the Romans, too. All they were doing was trying to keep the Pax Romana, the peace. They were honoring Rome's commitment to keep things smooth in that tiny satellite country under their protection. Does that make the Romans the bad guys?

Loving our enemy means seeing things from his or her side. It means listening to his or her hopes and fears. It means taking the time to learn what's right about what is wrong, and what's wrong about what is right — because we don't know which is wrong and which is right. We cannot distinguish the good buys from the bad guys. We just think we can.

When we hear the word *enemy*, we think *bad guys*. But enemy simply means opponent. It doesn't connote good or bad, right or wrong. It means the person opposed, that's all. God sends the sun and the rain on the good guys and on the bad guys, the righteous and the unrighteous — but God doesn't tell us which ones we are. God just wets and dries — all of us.

Consider Moses, our great lawgiver, great leader, great prophet, great mediator with God for us, great liberator — and great murderer, great fugitive from justice in Egypt where he was sought by a legitimate government. If you think about it, America isn't much different from either Egypt or Rome. We're trying to keep the peace and help weaker governments run their countries efficiently. Moses and Jesus, taken from the American viewpoint, would have been the bad guys. But somehow the Bible says it was through Moses and in Jesus that God revealed justice and salvation for the world. God tells us that these two are also *good guys* because God says so. It didn't matter how we judged them — good guys or bad guys — because God made them, Jesus and Moses, good guys.

If we are to love our enemies, as Christ commands, we've got to see things from the other side, even if just briefly. We've got to change our point of view, identify with a different character than usual.

Look at this story of Joseph and his brothers. We usually identify with Joseph, don't we? Today let's try to understand the position of the father and the brothers.

Joseph was Jacob's eleventh son, Dad's pet. Maybe he whined a lot to get his needs met, was a con artist. One day Dad gave him a fabulous coat, better than anything the others got. That burned their buns. The text says "they hated him, and could not speak peaceably to him."

Now remember, we're identifying not with Joseph but with the brothers this time. Young Joseph is a spoiled brat. He steals Dad's favor and tries to argue he has God's favor, too. Joseph has two dreams in which we brothers bow down to him, he says, so we hate him more. Then he tells Dad of another dream, after which Dad scolds him, saying, "What kind of a dream is this? Shall we indeed come, I and your mother and your brothers, and bow to the ground before you?" Our brother is an obnoxious 17-year-old.

Finally, we brothers have had enough. We plan to kill Joseph. He's wrecking the family. But Reuben suggests we throw Joseph into a pit instead. As we prepare to do that, a caravan passes by going to Egypt, so we sell Joseph into slavery. It's an easy out that also turns a profit.

If we look ahead, we see "Joseph was taken down to Egypt, and Potiphar, an officer of Pharaoh, the captain of the guard, an Egyptian, bought him ... The Lord was with Joseph" (Genesis 39:1-2a) With Joseph? The Lord with Joseph? What kind of God is this — hanging out with slaves?

Next Joseph worked his way up in Potiphar's household, probably whining and wheedling his way up the same way he did with Dad. He gets in a scrape with Potiphar's wife and lands in prison. But scripture says, in prison "the Lord was with Joseph" (v. 21). What kind of God is this who hangs around prisons? If the guy's a hero, why doesn't God just send out a medium-sized earthquake to knock down the prison walls so the good guys can escape? A real God, a living God, a God who solves people's problems — especially the problems of the good guys — could just blast those Commies, I mean Democrats, I mean Republicans, whoever, off the map. Sorry, I mean Egyptian guards. Yeah, that's it, God could just blast them off the face of the earth.

What a mixed-up God! What a mixed-up Bible! This is only Genesis, the first book of the Bible, yet God doesn't seem to clearly know who the good guys are and who the bad guys are. Look. God is with that egg-sucking, sweet-talking, finagling Joseph in prison. Next thing you know, we'll find God with a bunch of ignorant, dirty slaves who are making bricks in Egypt. And then we'll hear that God is with some rebellious kid born in a manger in a stable! And we'll probably see this same mixed-up God up on a cross with a teacher charged with blasphemy. What a mixed-up God! Can't even tell the good guys from the bad guys.

Remember what happened to Joseph? He started a seven-year grain storage program for Pharaoh, just before a famine hit the neighboring countries. Joseph stored so much grain that the Egyptians could supply everyone's needs.

Joseph will test his brothers' honesty in subsequent chapters when they make three trips to Egypt for grain. In a tearful reunion, Joseph will say, "I am your brother Joseph, whom you sold into Egypt. And now do not be distressed, or angry with yourselves, because you sold me here; for God sent me before you to preserve life" (Genesis 45:4-5). Joseph says it wasn't they who sent him to Egypt, but God.

What craziness! How can God take such evil, the evil of us selling our brother into slavery, and turn it into such good? How can God turn it into a blessing that will save us later?

As we saw in the story of Judas and the Romans, and again here in the story of Joseph, we're not sure who is good and who is bad. God sprinkles rain on both and shines sun on both. God loves all.

So the next question is: If God is God over good and bad, why doesn't God just eliminate the bad? How? By fighting evil with evil? That would suggest the Crusades and Holy Wars. "In the name of good, I cut off your head."

No, of course God wouldn't do it that way. God would take the evil out of the hearts of human beings, we say. Let everybody be good — no good guys, no bad, everybody good.

But whose good? The Communist good? The capitalist good? The Republican good? The Democratic good? The George Bush good, the Bill Clinton good, the Ross Perot good? The Moral Majority good, the David Koresh good? My good, your good? Obviously, good means good from *my* perspective. Not from God's, but from mine, or from yours.

A baby dies under a dump truck wheel, so we call it a strike against God. It cannot be good when a baby dies. But a starving baby dies at the very peak of Somalia's starvation, so we decide that some babies are better off dead. So now it's sometimes good when a baby dies. What's happened to our concept of good?

Herod and the Romans were trying to kill babies, too, all Hebrew babies under two years old, so they could stop the birth of the Messiah. Why didn't God just blast them off the face of the earth? One reason may have been that Herod and the Romans represented the responsible and legitimate political power of that time, and they were keeping the peace as well as it had been kept until then. Sounds like America, doesn't it? If Herod and the Romans — the peacekeepers — were the bad guys, who are the bad guys keeping the peace nowadays?

Can't we see that we sold our nasty little brother Joseph into slavery? Can't we see that we don't like being called the bad guys, even when we are? Can't we admit we're glad God doesn't blast bad guys off the face of the earth (or we'd be dust)? Can't we see that the ones we saw as bad guys — like manipulative, whiny Joseph, or murdering Moses — may turn out to be good guys? Can't we understand that the ones we saw as good guys (us) could indeed turn out to be the bad guys? Can't we see that *good guys* and *bad guys* are terms that depend on where we are standing? Can we see that loving our enemies means loving those who don't agree with us? That the enemy isn't necessarily bad — just opposite or opposed?

To be perfect as our heavenly Father is perfect means to love everyone, for God doesn't see enemies among us, just different people with different ideas. To paraphrase Jesus' words: "Love the good guys and the bad guys as I have loved you, so that you may be sons and daughters of the heavenly Father."

As We Forgive Those Who Trespass Against Us

A man got out of the Navy and planned to attend college. Before departing for the college town, though, he and his wife stopped by his parents' house in their old hometown so they could pick up a few items he'd left there in the attic — pictures from school days, bowling trophies, a high school letter sweater, and a coin collection.

The trouble came when the man couldn't find the coin collection that had been his joy growing up. He had collected nearly every Lincoln Head penny from 1909 on, including a rare 1909S VDB. He had Liberty dimes, Buffalo nickels, half a coin book filled with Indian Head pennies. He had Flying Eagle cents from the mid-1800s.

Trouble was, when he located the coin books in the attic, all of them were empty. He ranted and raved, shouted and screamed, then found out from his mother that his teenage brother had spent all the coins to buy booze. And he'd spent them *at face value, not at their estimated worth*!

Was that ex-sailor ever angry! So angry, in fact, that he told his parents — who seemed to know the teenage brother was already an alcoholic, but did nothing to stop him — told them that he'd never step foot in their house again so long

29

as the teenage brother was living under their roof and still drinking. He also vowed never to speak to his brother again until the brother quit drinking.

And he didn't ... for almost a year. The older brother's anger and indignation stuck with him that long.

But finally — finally — he realized that he was punishing his parents for his little brother's offense. He was angry about his brother's uncontrolled alcoholism, and he was hurt and angry because it had affected him now. But he gave up his anger as best he could and began to visit his parents again. He even spoke to his brother, though the drinking continued to be a major problem for another 20 years.

That ex-sailor did manage to forgive his younger brother for stealing and squandering the coin collection he loved. Now the ex-sailor is in his mid-40s, the brother in his mid-30s, and they're finally starting to develop a better relationship. What they've got is mainly because of forgiveness — on both sides. The older brother forgave the theft of the coins; the younger brother forgave the elder for the way he responded by hurting their parents.

There have been other hurts in that relationship, too, and other forgivenesses. Those brothers — and the rest of us in this world — couldn't operate without forgiveness. Life and relationships can't work without forgiveness.

You're late for an appointment. I've been waiting an hour-and-a-half. Where on earth have you been? I've been sitting here steaming — steaming because it's ungodly hot, and steaming because you didn't care enough about me to call and say you'd be late.

Stop the action.

I can get mad at you and stay mad at you. I have good reason. Obviously you were wrong and I was right. I can get mad and refuse to continue our relationship. I can refuse to ever speak to you again. I'll find other friends. *But I care about you. So I forgive you.* No, you *cannot* make it up to me; there's no way to turn back the clock and be on time for the appointment. Forgiveness is the only answer. I'll forgive you and we'll get on with our relationship.

See what I mean? We forgive one another all the time. It's usually for the small things, for the minor offenses. Sometimes it's for the bigger ones.

Remember the bus crash in Kentucky six or eight years ago? Dozens of children and several chaperones from a church youth group were killed when a pickup truck crossed the road and hit the bus, causing the bus to burst into flames. The parents of one of the children were willing to forego a cash settlement from the pickup's driver if the bus company would recall all the buses with similar gas tank designs so they could be fixed and made safer, so the same thing wouldn't happen to other children and chaperones. And they and another couple were willing to forgive the truck driver, even going so far as to ask the judge for a lenient penalty. That's costly forgiveness — for the offended party to not seek retaliation.

Forgiveness is a funny thing, hard for many of us to understand. It's not tit-for-tat, not action-reaction.

In the early 1960s talk was about missiles, and anti-missiles, and anti-missile-missiles, and anti-missile-missile-missiles. The underlying premise was that one country would shoot first, the other would have to retaliate, then the first country would have to retaliate for the retaliation, so the second country would have to retaliate for the retaliation to the retaliation . . . and so on *ad infinitum*. There's no end to it, no way to ever get even, is there? And through it all, both countries, millions of people, and the whole world — *everybody* — *suffers*. There's no real justice and no real sense to that, is there?

Take the Hatfield/McCoy feud of legend. A Hatfield kills a McCoy, so a McCoy has to go out and kill a Hatfield. But that doesn't really even the score, because every Hatfield knows a Hatfield is worth two McCoys, and every McCoy believes a McCoy is worth three Hatfields — so another death has to occur. There's no end, no stopping the bloodshed — until there's forgiveness. Someone has to say, "I'll keep carrying that last hurt, and I won't retaliate."

In today's scripture story, we see the reunion of Joseph and his brothers in Egypt. Remember, though, that it isn't as if they're all looking for each other. This isn't a case of brothers separated at birth and reunited after 70 years of searching and hiring private detectives. No, these are the brothers who sold young Joseph into slavery to get rid of him. These brothers did him wrong.

What's happened in the interim time, though, is that Joseph has risen to a position of the highest authority in Pharaoh's household. He's a bright fellow and, foreseeing some lean years for the country and surrounding countries, he has started a grain storage program. In a time of famine, his brothers come to Egypt for help. That's when the reunion occurs.

Note how they respond. They are silent, cowering, afraid of Joseph's retribution. Now that he's in a position of power and they in a position of need, the cast-off brother could retaliate. He could really sock it to them.

But he doesn't. Instead, he rejoices at seeing them. He makes the first move and hugs and kisses them. He's the offended party, but because they can't do anything to restore the relationship to health, he (Joseph) must make the first move. (It's similar to the New Testament parable Jesus tells about the Prodigal Son who has squandered his inheritance. He comes back to his Father without a leg to stand on, having hurt their relationship — and it is the Father who acts first to restore the relationship to health.) In the case of the Prodigal Son and his Father, and in the case of Joseph and his brothers, the relationship was important enough to warrant forgiveness — but the cost of the forgiving must be borne by the offended party. It's what we call the "double burden."

Yes, it is a pain to keep forgiving, because there are so many little indiscretions we commit, so many sins, so many hurts we inflict on others. We grate on one another; we stick to our opinions so firmly at times that we steamroll others; we neglect others, thereby hurting them. Sometimes it's inadvertent, sometimes deliberate. Regardless, we do offend and hurt other people. That seems to be the nature of being in relationships.

So how many times must we forgive? Peter asks Jesus, "So how about seven?" That seems to be a meaningful number.

But Jesus responds by saying, "Seven? How about seventy times seven?" Just the tone of his voice must have implied that a limit was ridiculous. So long as we are living, we must keep on forgiving, because we keep offending.

That's not to say there's no limit or that we have to be naive about offering forgiveness. There are abusive, dead-end situations where one hurt follows right on the heels of another, and the one doing the hurting shows no signs of repentance or remorse at all. Some people will simply take advantage of the situation. So there are limits at times.

And then there's repentance which has to be considered. Forgiveness is a device, a mechanism, we need in order to restore a broken relationship to health; it's not giving in or saying, "Forget it," just to make peace, to avoid conflict. But forgiveness isn't complete, and the relationship isn't restored to health, without true and sincere repentance that accompanies the acceptance of forgiveness.

Joseph's brothers repent. They repent and accept the forgiveness offered them. That's why this reunion is so potent and the tears flow so freely. Both sides want to restore this relationship. Yes, Joseph made the first move, but the brothers had to act, too. (Maybe Joseph even asked their forgiveness for being such a jerk during the years he was growing up at home.)

In Jeremiah 33 we see God has promised to forgive *our* iniquity and remember (that's to bring to mind, to dredge up and hold against) *our* sin no more. So the offer is out there; the first action is taken by the offended party, God. God forgives us. It is up to us to repent and accept that forgiveness.

In the Lord's Prayer we ask, "Forgive us our trespasses as we forgive those who trespass against us." If we want to maintain a healthy relationship with God, if we expect God to forgive us our offenses daily, we must also forgive those who have hurt us. We don't owe it to them, but we must see that restoring a relationship to health is not in *their* power. Only we who are the offended can do it.

As the ex-sailor did for his coin-stealing brother, as Joseph did for his back-stabbing brothers, as the Father did for his wayward Prodigal Son — *as God has done for us* — we too must be generous in exercising forgiveness.

To see the generosity, the sheer extravagance, of forgiveness, look at Jesus. Hanging there nailed to a cross, hard as it is to imagine, he says with his last breaths of life, "Father, forgive them. They know not what they do."

Forgiveness — unmerited, but necessary — the dearest gift we can ever give. Or receive. Let us thank God for showing us such a gift with which to heal.

God's Power Over Death

Unto a woman is born a child, Moses. But the timing is unfortunate, for this is at a time when Pharaoh has ordered all newborn Hebrew males thrown into the Nile. So Moses' mother hides him for three months until she cannot hide him any longer. She's got her back against the wall, knows she's got to do something, and that's when she and her daughter (Moses' sister) cook up this plan.

They waterproof a wicker cradle to transform it into a miniature Noah's Ark. Into it goes baby Moses. They place the wicker basket in the reeds at the water's edge, making it appear that it's washed up by an act of providence. The mother and the sister are aware that the Pharaoh's daughter, the princess, regularly bathes there, so they are fairly confident she'll find the infant Moses.

But here's the drama. What'll this princess do upon finding the babe in the basket? She's an Egyptian and, perhaps even worse, she's Pharaoh's daughter. Will she defy her father's directive? Will she push the cradle out into the Nile and watch it either sink below the surface or float downstream? Will she summon her guards? What will the princess do? Moses' mother and sister, after they leave the basket in the reeds at the river's edge, try to console each other and try to convince themselves to trust in God.

Sis is a little less trusting, apparently, and, according to scripture, stands "at a distance to see what would be done to him." She peeks anxiously through the high weeds at the princess' party.

Moses' mother is so worked up she can't bear to watch, so she waits at home, saying her prayers and trying not to cry. It's awful, and the waiting for news hurts. What will the princess do?

The princess sees the basket and sends her maid to fetch it. When she opens it, the baby is crying. She feels sorry for him and holds him in her arms and rocks him just as you or I would have done. She knows full well this is a Hebrew child, for she says aloud in a voice that Moses' sister can hear, "This is one of the Hebrews' children."

Uh-oh. Sis, maybe spur-of-the-moment or maybe as part of a plan, leaps out of the bushes and blurts out, "Shall I get you a wet nurse?"

The princess, who in all likelihood can see through the holes in this plan, can say no. She can choose to obey her father the Pharaoh and have this baby killed. But she looks at the crying Moses, and she looks at the pleading of Moses' sister's eyes, and she nods at the girl and says, "Go."

No need to tell Moses' sister twice. She's gone, leaving only a trail of dust in her wake. As she nears home, she starts yelling out the good news to her mother, "Mama, mama! He's okay, he's alive! And she needs a wet nurse. You, his own mother, can be his wet nurse!"

Moses' mother springs to her feet and dashes back toward the river bank, arriving out of breath and trying to gasp out the words, "I'm a wet nurse; I'm a wet nurse," at the princess. Imagine her joy when the princess hands her the baby, and when Moses' mother puts him to her breast. It's actually sort of a resurrection story, isn't it — an Old Testament account of God's restoring one's life?

Think about it. When we human beings are faced with the threat of our own death or the death of a loved one, how do we react? Generally, we try desperately either to extend life or to learn what is beyond — that is, we seek knowledge; we've got to know. We feel helpless, powerless. So what can help us? Maybe a peek at God's power over Death.

Here's another story, this one from our present day, and true.

Todd was two months into pastoring his first church. He'd served communion once, never done a baptism or funeral.

The hospital's patient listing showed a 22-year-old from Todd's parish area admitted to intensive care. Todd didn't know the name, but he knew enough to visit anyone from his area.

The boy's name was Gary, and his spinal cord had been severed in a car accident. He was paralyzed from the neck down and couldn't speak. When Todd saw him that first day, Gary had breathing devices and IV tubes everywhere. It wasn't a good time to talk, so Todd said hello and left, feeling helpless.

Over the next month Todd visited Gary daily.

One night Gary's mother called Todd from the hospital. The doctors gave Gary less than two days to live. Todd left for the hospital.

When he arrived, Gary's mother fell into Todd's arms and wept. Todd wept, too, and felt even more powerless to affect things now. He asked if the doctors had told Gary he was dying. They said no and asked if Todd would tell him. He agreed before he could think twice.

"Gary," Todd said, "I want you to know that God loves you. In the Bible there's a promise of eternal life. It's there and I believe it. Somehow, I believe it. But it's hard to read it and not know it through feeling it in your heart. But right now I feel it; I know it. And it tells me that nothing — not life, nor death, nor anything else in all of creation — can separate us in a love like ours — mine, yours, and God's." They were both crying now. "As a friend, I've got to be honest with you, Gary — you're going to die." Todd's own words cut through his heart like a burning knife. But Gary seemed glad to know finally. They cried more and Todd went to Gary's mother.

"We don't know what'll happen to Gary," she said. "Jesus will have to decide."

"What do you mean?" Todd asked.

"Gary's never been baptized," she said.

"I can do it," Pastor Todd said without flinching.

"Gary, do you want to be baptized?" Todd asked. Gary nodded yes with his eyes, so Todd stepped to the nurse's station.

"Could I have some water?" he asked. "It's for a baptism."

The nurse filled a plastic cough medicine cup to the brim with water and handed it to Todd. He took it to Gary's room.

"Gary," Todd asked, not knowing any of the words to the liturgy for the baptismal service, "Do you profess Jesus Christ as your Lord and Savior?" Gary's eyes nodded yes. "Then I baptize you into the Christian faith in the name of the Father, the Son, and the Holy Ghost." And with that Pastor Todd poured the medicine cup of water back over Gary's forehead where it ran down through his brown, tousled hair.

Suddenly, in a time of no hope and numbing, paralyzing fear, there was hope, and the three of them broke out in broad smiles and laughed and wept with joy. In that instant the three of them knew in their hearts the truth of the resurrection and its hope.[1]

Back to the question we started with. When we're faced with death — our own or the death of a loved one — our human response is either to try desperately to extend life or to learn what's beyond (knowledge, assurances). We're often paralyzed by fear.

What then shall we do? We must watch for signs of God's power, power even over Death, for we can then draw strength from those incidents. They can help us to have faith.

Here's a third story. It comes from the New Testament (John 20:11-18). Mary Magdalene has gone to the tomb where

Jesus' body has been laid after the crucifixion. She is weeping so hard that she mistakes the risen Christ for a gardener. After a few moments, she recognizes her Lord, and he tells her to announce to his brothers that he is ascending to the Father. Then the text says, "Mary Magdalene went and announced to the disciples, 'I have seen the Lord. I have seen the Lord.' " Again, Death has no power over our God, my friends.

Moses' mother and sister might have chosen to explain away God's saving act, but they didn't, recalling instead that miraculous moment when Moses was put to his own mother's breast — God's power over death. Seen through the eyes of faith, it gave them strength and hope.

Pastor Todd, Gary, and Gary's mother might have rationalized away the miraculous joy of the moment of Gary's baptism, when hope sprang forth. But they didn't. They, too, caught a glimpse of God's awesome power, power even over Death. They understood the experience through the eyes of faith.

Mary Magdalene, at the tomb on Easter morn, saw with the eyes of faith, too. She caught a vision of God's power over Death, and it changed her life in such a way that she then went forth and changed the lives of others.

We, too, might explain away those moments when God's power over Death is revealed. But we mustn't. We must look for them, witness to them and their transformative power, and keep telling our stories — the way Moses' mother and sister did, the way Pastor Todd and Gary's mother did, the way Mary Magdalene and the disciples did. God is repeatedly and continually working powerful miracles in our lives. We must see them through the eyes of faith, and as a people of God, we must share the wonder of our God with the world.

---

1. Steve Burt, "The Power Of The Resurrection Over Death," *56 Lectionary Stories For Preaching* (Lima, Ohio: CSS Publishing, 1993), pp. 51-52.

What Do You Say To A Burning Bush?

The Moses I always pictured is the Charlton Heston Moses, the one who leads his people out of Egypt, who parts the Red Sea, gives commands. But the Moses we hear and see in today's scripture reading is different, not the heroic, bigger-than-life character. He's tending sheep, but to see how he got there we must look back to Exodus 2:11-15.

A nutshell summary goes like this. Moses is standing around, observes a fight, and kills an Egyptian. We can't just write that Egyptian off as somebody who doesn't count. Fact is, Moses has killed someone. So we have a Moses we don't often think about: a murderer who covers his crime by stuffing the body in the sand so nobody will find out. He tries to hide his sin, cover the fact that he's a murderer.

Moses is a fugitive. He leaves Egypt, flees to Midian. He's on Egypt's 10 Most Wanted List, hiding out. He becomes a shepherd, a new profession for a new identity. There's nothing glamorous about the job, and it's not the cleanest work in the world.

So Moses is a murderer and a fugitive from justice. He's dirty, sweaty, smells of sheep, and arrives at this place on the barren north forty where he has taken the flock to graze. He's up to his ankles in sheep muck.

41

Picture it. There's nothing holy about that place. No shrine, no temple. So Moses, this unlikely candidate who is certainly not a saint, stumbles his way into this unlikely place that's surely not one of the world's major highways, and suddenly this burning bush flames up. It fires his curiosity. Not enough that a bush burns mysteriously, but then the darned thing has to go and call his name, saying, "Moses. Moses." Two times to get his attention.

There's something about somebody calling our names that makes us pay attention. It could mean life or death, particularly if we're crossing the street at the time. The person who calls out my name holds power over me. I look.

Next comes an invitation to make contact, physical contact. "Moses, take off your shoes." Too often, I think, we interpret this to mean, "Take off your shoes so you don't *defile* God." If that were the case, though, we'd leave our shoes on, because our smelly feet would be even more offensive than our sandals, wouldn't they? Consider instead that this may be an invitation to *make contact*. God, who in later years would come among us as Jesus, isn't worried about remaining antiseptically perfect. God wants to come and be with us, to *make* contact, not to avoid it.

Now think about this. Holiness doesn't depend on the condition of the place nor the condition of the person. Holiness, to be hallowed, depends on the presence of God.

That's why this church — and it doesn't matter whether you use the word "church" to mean the building or the people — isn't necessarily holy on its own. What makes it holy is the presence of God. Same with that little stable in Bethlehem; what made it holy was the presence of God at the birth of a child. That's why a crucifixion can be something through which salvation is offered. What's holy is not the timbers, the nails, or the spectators. What's holy is God's presence in the event.

"Take off your shoes, Moses. Take off your shoes and come into direct contact with me. Touch me. Experience me." It's like God says, "Maybe I'll give you a foot rub, a massage.

Feel the warmth of my holy hands on your toes, Moses. It's been a long, hard road for you, Moses. Relax. And don't worry. I'm not afraid of your dirty, tired feet." Remember Jesus washing his disciples' feet?

God says, "Take off your shoes, Moses. I know you've got dirt between your toes. Everybody does. I know you've got it under your toenails that are probably too long and curling over. I know that as sure as I know about every single hair on your head. I'm God. And I know, Moses, that you're a murderer and a fugitive. I know all about you. I'm God — the God of Abraham, Isaac, and Jacob. I created the heavens and the earth in the beginning. I created you and all this mess. I take full responsibility. Now sit down, take off your shoes, Moses, and spend some time with me, will ya?" Holiness doesn't depend on the place's purity or the person's purity; it depends on the presence of God.

After sitting a while, Moses is asked by his new-found friend God, who is rubbing his feet, "Do something for me, will you, Moses? You labored and were heavy-laden and I gave you a foot rub after you'd been herding sheep all day long. Now listen, my people in Egypt are suffering from heat, overwork, exhaustion, dehydration, loss of liberty — and I feel for them. Go and help them, will you, Moses? Tell them I sent you. I'll be with you. You won't see me, and that's the tough part, Moses. You won't see me any more than you see me now, but I'll be with you. I promise."

Moses, nervous, thinks, "I knew I shouldn't have taken my shoes off, shouldn't have gone for the foot rub, shouldn't have rubbed elbows with God. What was I to think? After all, God knew my name and called me. I had to answer. It'd be impolite not to."

So Moses answers God something like this. "Well, golly, God, I'll look like a fool — saying you sent me, especially if you're not visible. They'll say, 'We don't see him.' Darn it, what'll I do to prove it was you who sent me?"

God answers, "You can try a few magic tricks, Moses. Probably won't convince them — never has before. In the

43

end you can only say, 'God sent me,' and they'll either believe it or they won't. I'm not asking you, Moses, to guarantee they'll buy it; I'm just asking you, Moses, as a friend, to do me a favor. Just go and tell the people I care. Maybe they'll even follow if you lead.''

Moses keeps hemming and hawing like when a friend asks you to do something personally uncomfortable to you — you know, after you say, "If there's anything I can do, anything at all'' — and they take you up on it?

Moses thinks, "God, why this, of all things? Why did you ask me to go back into Egypt where I'm a fugitive? There's a price on my head. It's a long trip. It's hot.''

That's what Moses *thinks*, but how does he answer? He says, "Well, God, I'd really like to help you. I really would, old buddy.'' Then he jumps onto a legitimate disability he has, rather than lie. "I can't speak very well, God. Honest. I stutter and I stammer. I mean I ssstutter and I stam-stam-stam-stammer. See?''

To that, God replies, "I know that, Moses. After all, I am the one who made your mouth. I know the inside of it better than your orthodontist does. And you're stuck with it. I'm not changing it at this late date. After all, I'm not a magician nor an orthodontist — I'm God. Take your brother Aaron along. He'll follow you. He'd love to try public speaking. He's a ham and enjoys getting up in front of crowds. Take a gamble, Moses. I'll be with both of you.''

Moses says to the bush, "C'mon, God, give me a break.''

And, flaming up slightly, the burning bush answers, "Moses, I've just about had it with you. I've answered your objections. Now I'm asking you, as a friend — and don't forget, the foot rub was free — Will you go and help my people, carry the message to them that I still care about them? I love them, Moses.''

At that Moses walks away mumbling, "Boy, that was a darned expensive foot rub.'' But he goes. He goes off into history, off into our Bible, and off into movies, providing work for Charlton Heston.

Greek has two different words for time. The first is *kronos,* from which we get *chronology.* It is measured time. The second is *kairos.* It might be translated as *event time,* almost a magical, mystical, timeless time.

Whereas time and life are *measured* in minutes and seconds according to *kronos,* much of life is *lived* on *kairos* or event time. *Kronos* says time is a stream of even-sized droplets; *kairos* says it's more like the islands in a stream, each a different size and consistency, each providing a different adventure or experience. There are other important islands in the stream along life's way, too: retreats, vacations, graduations, nativity pageants, recitals — all on *kairos* time, not equally weighted. Moses' time with God might have been five minutes or five hours or five days. The burning bush experience was *kairos* time.

And *kairos* time is often holy time. It's holy not because of the purity of the people or the purity of the place, but because God is present in those events. And when God is present, there is hope.

Vermont writer/pastor Steve Burt describes a burning bush experience. "I remember my daughter Wendy's junior high prom. One minute she was in eighth grade, and the next she was making the transition into ninth grade, high school. In no time she'd be graduating. But, oh, that junior high prom. That expensive gown we didn't really have the money for. Those special new shoes she just had to have — ah, how they turned her into Cinderella when she slipped them on.

"I drove Wendy and her date (a boy six inches shorter than she), and the other couple they were going with, to the restaurant where they'd first have dinner.

"I made them stand outside in the parking lot so I could capture that *kairos* event on Kodak. As I aimed through the viewfinder, I found myself suddenly looking at a burning bush, a flaming tree that put even Vermont's fall foliage to shame. I don't know whether it was the blush on Wendy's cheeks or the flash of the camera — I don't know what it was, but here was something that hadn't been on fire before. She was on fire now. Yet she wasn't consumed, nor was I. God was present, and I was standing on holy ground.

"The place wasn't particularly holy, a restaurant parking lot. The persons weren't particularly holy. We weren't murderers like Moses, but we had, no doubt, in the last couple of minutes or days or weeks, said murderous things about people. We weren't holy people. But I could see and feel God's presence. I could see and feel the heat.

"It was *my* daughter growing up, yet she wasn't *my* child; she was a child of the world, a child of hope, the child in the Bethlehem manger with all the animals breathing their hot breath to warm her in the hay. Perhaps she'd be the one to do better than I in life, the one who would make a difference in the world on God's behalf.

"In that moment, as I saw her burning brightly, I had hope that she would grow up in a world of peace, where the lion lies down with the lamb and they both get a good night's sleep, where we don't live in fear, where there's enough food for everybody and meaningful employment for all to enjoy their work. Somehow, in that restaurant parking lot on Eastern Daylight Kairos Time, I heard the invitation, 'Steve, you're on holy ground, not because of the place or the people, but because I am here.' I beheld my daughter in her junior high prom dress, I beheld God's handiwork, and it was good. God was saying, 'Rough day as a shepherd, pastor? Enjoy the view, take off your shoes, relax. Enjoy being in touch with me. You can't look directly into my face. Moses couldn't. But I've given you a miracle to focus on instead, a burning bush, a daughter in a prom dress.'

"I did. I enjoyed being in the presence of God, and I came away different, as we always do.

" 'Where do I go from here?' I asked myself.

"God answered, 'I'm glad you asked.'

"To which I replied, 'Oh-oh.'

" 'Well,' God said. 'It's like this. Just tell my people I love them and I know their suffering. I'm not blind, nor callous, nor insensitive. Tell them that what makes a place holy isn't the real estate or the clientele; I can take care of that. I can make a sheep pasture, a parking lot, a manger, even a cross on a hillside — I can make all of those places holy just by being there. Tell them. I'll be with you, and with them. I promise.' "

Friends, it's true. God loves us, cares about us, knows our pains and sufferings and secret sins. Despite those sins, God loves us and is not distant. When God says, "Come unto me, all ye who labor and are heavy-laden, and I will give you rest," God isn't kidding. Our God gives great foot rubs.

May our lives be filled with burning bushes so that we come into contact with God and experience holy ground.

Proper 18
Pentecost 16
Ordinary Time 23
Exodus 12:1-14

Jesus Christ, Our Passover Lamb

In the summer of 1976 a hurricane approached eastern Long Island, New York. Older residents recalled the 1938 hurricane which had claimed many lives and destroyed millions of dollars worth of property. Even the younger residents could remember the devastation wreaked by Hurricanes Donna, Carol, and others in the 1950s and 1960s. People took seriously the warnings of the National Weather Service; they battened down the hatches, stored bottled water, provisions, and candles in basements, and prepared for the worst. One man offered this account.

"When the hurricane hit, around dusk, the sky turned black. The swirling wind picked up dust and loose leaves and anything it could find, pelting the house. Sheets of black rain raced across the fields like an army of shadowy soldiers coming to overrun our position. We retreated to the cellar and sat it out for a couple of hours, hearing the noise of battle above us, wondering what would be left of what we cared about above us. Eventually, it was over. It wasn't as bad as predicted. It was bad, though, and there was a lot of damage. One man in the next town was killed by a falling tree limb. But it wasn't like the hurricane of '38 or even '54 or '56, thank God."[1]

It's not difficult for us to imagine that man's experience or to picture what it's like to huddle in a tornado shelter. Maybe that's what it felt like in London during the blitz — people huddled together in bomb shelters, never knowing when the bombs would hit or where, wondering whose home would be destroyed next, worrying about family and friends across town. Would this be the night tragedy struck *our* household?

It must have felt like that to the Hebrews living in Egypt 3,000 years ago. They were slaves, making bricks and dragging stones to erect the monuments Pharaoh Ramses II was so intent on building. It was to these Hebrew slaves that God sent Moses with the instruction (in the words of the old spiritual): "Let my people go." Ramses didn't want to hear it, though, and told Moses (indirectly, God) to take a hike.

Well, Moses reported back to God with the bad news. So God sent Pharaoh a Nasty-gram, a plague. In fact, each time Pharaoh refused to let the people go, another plague was visited on the land of Egypt. The river Nile turned blood red, frogs infested the land, everybody got lice, flies worse than black-flies swarmed over people, cattle dropped dead in the streets, everybody got boils on their bodies, hail destroyed the crops, and locusts ate whatever the hail didn't ruin. Finally, the lights went out when there was an eclipse of the sun.

But Pharaoh had seen plagues before, and the Egyptian people had survived worse than this. Then came the worst night of all, the most horrible Egypt would ever endure, a night for weeping and gnashing of teeth. A deadly plague visited the land, and cries of misery and mourning were everywhere as each family's firstborn son lay stricken and dying. It was an awful, terrifying night unlike any other night in their history — worse perhaps than the hurricane, the tornado, or the London blitz. There was no way to fight back and nowhere to hide. It must have been oh-so-painful for those Egyptians who lost children, and it must have been frightening for the Hebrews who cowered inside their houses, praying God would keep the promise and pass over the homes where they'd smeared lamb's blood on the doorposts. We've all had those long, dark nights, haven't we — what Meister Eckhardt called "the dark night of the soul"?

Scott Peck's book, *The Road Less Traveled*, begins with the line, "Life is difficult." Life *is* indeed difficult much of the time, occasionally even downright cruel. We've all had our own long, dark nights — the loss of a loved one that was so painful, a physical disability that stopped us from being athletic, an injury or disease, a cancer that scared the very life out of us, a shattered dream, the breakup of a marriage and accompanying feelings of failure. Life is difficult. At times the dark night is very long.

Robert Veniga wrote a book titled *A Gift of Hope*, in which he interviewed survivors of the skywalk collapse at the Hyatt Regency in Kansas City some years ago. One woman, who lost her husband and two of her friends when the 65-ton steel structure came crashing to the ground, says even now, years later, she is startled by noise. Another survivor is wary of buildings with high ceilings, exposed beams, and overhead structures. She now checks out every building she enters, and once, finding herself on a balcony, she ran back into the building in panic. The dark night of the soul can be so, so long.

A woman, speaking several years after her husband's death, said, "It wasn't at the funeral that I experienced Howard's death. It was five months later, when I tried to decorate the Christmas tree alone." Life is difficult.

In this scripture lesson we see the story of the Hebrew slaves in Egypt on the night of the Passover. They knew how difficult life could be — they were born into it. Moses knew it for he was born into it as well. His mother saved his life by placing him in a basket in the bulrushes so Pharaoh's daughter would discover and raise him. Moses' mother had to do it, because the Pharaoh had ordered the firstborn male baby in each Hebrew family killed. So that's the context for the story of the first Passover — a difficult and sometimes cruel world.

Even though we in this present day read daily of the slaughter of thousands upon thousands in "trouble spots" around the world, you and I still live more protected lives than those Hebrew slaves 3,000 years ago. But we live in America, and we've been somewhat insulated from much of the savagery that characterizes parts of our modern world. Still, we can never be completely insulated. Even in our area we have murders, people drown, others are killed by drunk drivers, all causing immeasurable pain and grief. The night can be terribly long.

But even in the face of that, we are a people who have chosen to place our faith in God. In a symbolic way we are the people today who have painted our doorposts with the blood of the sacrificed lamb. As Christians we can't miss the parallel symbolism here. Jesus Christ, the Lamb of God who takes away the sins of the world, makes us the beneficiaries of a new Passover, a Passover from the tragedies of sin and death.

That's not to say bad times and trouble will always pass by us. It doesn't mean all smooth sailing. Brer Rabbit said, "You can't run away from trouble. Ain't no place that far." We can't run away from it nor can we hide from it.

The Hebrews' troubles didn't end the night of the Passover. They headed out and wandered the wilderness for 40 years. They had a peck of troubles. Life is, always will be, difficult.

In a movie called *Innerspace* a man and the capsule he is in are shrunk down to the size of a pinhead and injected into someone's body. All goes well for a while, and he smoothly pilots the craft around inside the body. Suddenly there's a fight, and the full-size person's blood pressure goes way up as his adrenaline gets pumping. The heart beats faster and faster, and the blood really rushes.

The tiny fellow in the capsule feels as if he's in an earthquake, and suddenly his craft gets sucked into the bloodstream so that he's heading at breakneck speed for the heart. It's like being sucked down a drain, and he's trying desperately to shoot grappling hooks out to catch them on an arterial wall. He desperately needs something to hold onto.

We've all been there at times, haven't we? Swirling around, trying to find something to hold onto. Life is hard. We want to pray with the Psalmist: "Do not hide your face from me, or I shall be like those who go down to the Pit" (Psalm 143). There are days when it feels like God is hiding both face and favor from us.

In *Uncle Tom's Cabin*, George Harris, a slave, says of slavetraders, "They buy us and sell us, and make trade of our heart's blood and groans and tears, and God lets them, He does; GOD LETS THEM."[2]

God doesn't let them. It may feel that way to George Harris. But God doesn't let them. God is always watching out for a Moses or a Martin Luther King to challenge the taskmasters and declare, "Let my people go." But sometimes it appears as if God lets it happen. The Psalmist not only writes, "Do not hide your face from me," but adds: "Let me hear of your steadfast love in the morning, *for in you I put my trust*" (Psalm 143).

In you I put my trust, O God. Life can be difficult, but we are the people who trust God. We are the ones who have smeared the blood of the lamb on our doorposts, who have taken refuge in the sacrificed lamb. We are the ones who have placed our confidence in a God who never forgets nor forsakes us.

The last part is this. Yes, life is difficult. But we who have placed our faith in God *will not be disappointed*! As the Apostle Paul said so powerfully:

> *If God is for us, who is against us? He who did not withhold his own Son, but gave him up for all of us, will he not with him also give us everything else? Who will separate us from the love of Christ? Will hardship, or distress, or persecution, or famine, or nakedness, or peril, or sword? No, in all these things we are more than conquerors through him who loved us. For I am convinced that neither death, nor life, nor angels, nor rulers, nor things present, nor things to come, nor powers, nor*

height, nor depth, nor anything else in all creation, will be able to separate us from the love of God in Christ Jesus our Lord. (Romans 8)

No matter how dark the night we will not be disappointed. The Hebrews knew nothing could separate them from the love of God and we know it, too, for we are people of the Passover and of the New Covenant in Christ Jesus.

---

1. Steve Burt, sermon preached in United Methodist Church, White River Junction, Vermont, July 26, 1987.

2. Harriet Beecher Stowe, *Uncle Tom's Cabin.*

Proper 19
Pentecost 17
Ordinary Time 24
Exodus 14:19-31

Need Help Removing That Roadblock?

A middle-aged man lived in a small town. He was single and had lived there all his life. Employment opportunities were limited, so he plucked chickens, a job he'd always hated. He secretly longed to be an artist, a painter.

The man prayed something might change to allow his dream of freedom to become realized — freedom from poverty and freedom to create. He felt as if invisible chains bound the true person he suspected was inside him.

One day a lawyer called from a nearby city and said the man was to receive an inheritance from a distant relative who had died overseas. The lawyer said it wouldn't make the man instantly rich; he couldn't even disclose whether the inheritance was money, but it *might* be. According to the terms of the will, it could only be revealed when he signed the papers. The lawyer said it would probably be worth the drive.

That's all he would have to do, drive to the city, sign the paper, and the inheritance that was *rightfully* his would *be actually* his. Then he'd be free to use it. Excited about the possibility he might be financially and creatively free, the man quit his chicken plucking job and headed for the city.

Halfway there he came to a sign that said ROAD CLOSED TO VEHICLES, FOOT TRAFFIC ONLY. There was no suggested detour and, since he wasn't familiar with the area, he had no idea what might be an alternate route. He had no map, no money, and he doubted he had the gas to drive a longer way.

So he sat there, staring at the sign that had become a roadblock to his dreams, the city still 20 to 30 miles away. He began to wonder if it was worth it. The road sign wasn't his only roadblock.

"After all," a voice in his head said, "the lawyer didn't say it was a 'large' or even a 'substantial' inheritance. And you didn't have a close relationship with that relative. You didn't even know him, so there's no reason to believe you were 'beloved' enough to 'deserve' a large gift. If you hurry back to town, maybe you can get your old job back. Things weren't so bad, were they?"

The man fought off the thoughts and considered making a go of it on foot. He imagined the walk would be hot and dry, and he had no water with him, nor was there a guarantee he'd find water along the way.

In his mind he pictured a chasm four or five miles ahead, a rope bridge spanning it, bridge swaying in the wind. If there was a chasm, and if there was a rope bridge, the ropes might be frayed or rotten, dangerous. He could fall to his death, losing the inheritance and his freedom. Even if he got across safely, he might be run down by wolves. Or step on a snake. For what? An inheritance that might be a few bucks and two ugly lamps for his end tables?

He thought about the job he had just quit. "It's not all that bad. Pays the rent, puts food on the table. It's backbreaking work, but it's steady. Maybe it's not as bad as I thought. And even if the inheritance money is enough to allow me to not work at a regular job while I create art, who says my art would be good? People might laugh at it."

But instead of turning the car around, he prayed, "God, if you can, help me to remove the roadblock." When he opened his eyes, a backpacker stepped up to the car.

"Going through?" the young hiker asked.

"Can't," the man replied. "It's closed."

"To vehicles," the hiker said. "We can walk together."

The man sat considering his options. What to do? What would you do if you were in his place?

We all face roadblocks to freeing the true self, don't we? There is a promise within us, a present if you will, that needs to be unwrapped. There's an authentic soul within each of us, maybe like the "self-actualized" human being which Erik Erikson describes. Or it could mean what mythologist Joseph Campbell is pointing to when he says, "Follow your bliss." Each of us has seen glimpses of that person deep inside ourselves. Some of us are more successful than others at nurturing it, freeing it, developing it. But there are roadblocks.

Roadblocks come in all different shapes and sizes. Some, like the ROAD CLOSED sign, come from outside. Others come from society, from truisms and negative myths, from people who don't realize they are squashing the dreams we have about fulfilling the promise within. Take the innocent comment to a six-year-old plinking away on a church piano: "Not bad, honey, but you'll never be a concert pianist."

Other internal roadblocks pop up like dandelions in spring. Self-doubts and temptations to abandon that quest abound. They appear as low self-esteem or self-deceptions, as a voice that says, "Ahh, I'll never play Carnegie Hall, so why play at all." (As if Carnegie Hall is the only place worth playing, and a living room isn't okay or enjoyable.)

Sad to say, some of these roadblocks are put or kept in place by parents, colleagues, teachers, ministers, society as a whole — by people whose opinions we value — so it is very hard to break free. It's harder than swimming upstream.

Consider this roadblock. Our American society is built on the ideals of success, social achievement, monetary success and security. Society pushes us to set aside dreams in order to "get a good-paying job so you can support your family . . . so you can be secure in retirement . . . so you'll be viewed as a respectable member of the community." God help you if you want to be a potter, a painter, a clown, because then you'll hear subtle and not-so-subtle messages cautioning, "You don't want to do that, child. You can't make a living at it. You're better off doing (blank)." A diverting action moves us away from our true selves.

Or how about this, the roadblock that devalues one's true calling. "Not a bad drawing, kid. But art is a hobby, not a job." Or substitute music. "Nice tune you wrote, sweetie. But music is a leisure activity, not a calling."

Whatever the roadblocks, whether they're placed there by others or by ourselves, we need to recognize there's an authentic person inside each of us whom God calls us to be.

Michelangelo, when asked how he envisioned the beautiful sculpture he'd chiseled from a huge block of marble, said, "There's an angel in there, and I've got to set it free." He chipped away whatever wasn't angel.

The Hebrew slaves, given a vision of freedom by Moses, escape their Egyptian taskmasters. They make the initial break from where they've been enslaved, like the chicken plucker. They met a roadblock, the Red Sea, and they sit, having in mind nothing more than a promise and a dream, a fuzzy idea about an inheritance that's theirs if they'll go and claim it. The inheritance *might* free them to be the authentic people God is calling them to be. To find out they'll have to trust and risk, for the Red Sea is menacing, an awesome roadblock. But the worst roadblocks bubble up from within. We can imagine the conversation.

A man says, "We'll never get across."

Someone adds, "The chariots are right on our tail. They'll rip us to shreds in the morning."

Another voice, "At least we'll die free."

An older woman says, "Maybe Moses didn't really talk to God; maybe he's leading us on a wild goose chase; perhaps we should abandon this silly dream."

Her friend chimes in, "If we surrender and go back, they won't kill us. They need us as slaves. We know what it's like behind us. We have no idea what lies ahead."

A gray-haired man says, "How did we ever get into this mess in the first place? Our friends who stayed behind told us this was foolish."

A lad of 13 replies boldly, "But I believe I am called to raise sheep, excellent, healthy sheep, not to be a slave making bricks and dragging huge stones for pyramids. It is for me and for my children and for my children's children that we left in the middle of the night, so that together we can be the people our God has called us to be."

Can we blame them, friends? Maybe it made more sense to go back, to return to a place that was at least *known* and thereby, oddly, *secure*. Like plucking chickens. "If I apologize, I can have my old job back. If I'm willing to re-bury my authentic, God-called self, I can feel more secure. Better than a risky, unknown, uncertain future." Besides, the Egyptian army is on the trail. The path forward looks closed. "Every time we try, we're defeated."

Like the man at the roadblock, the Hebrews turn to prayer. O God, we're following your calling for us, but there's a roadblock — the huge Red Sea. Please move it? (Of course, they don't really expect that kind of help.)

Now stop and think about that request. The Red Sea isn't the real roadblock, is it? The real roadblock shows up in their conversations. It's the self-doubts; it's the temptation to abandon the calling, the dream. It's the temptation to exchange the seeming security of what's behind for the promise ahead. Yes, the Red Sea is a major roadblock, but the real blocks are inside. Risk is scary.

I'm reminded of a person who, at age 44, discovered he might like to play the piano. He was scared and the road ahead promised lots of practice hours and hard work. He said to a friend, "I don't know about this. Have you any idea how old I'll be when I learn to play?" The friend replied, "Same age as if you don't?" The man took lessons. Risking — in order to follow that dream, to nurture that angel God has placed within us — that's often scary.

So Moses speaks to God, and God promises to be with them. God *wants* them to succeed, just as God wants that chicken plucker to become the artist he yearns to become. Once the Hebrews commit to becoming their true selves, slaves no longer — once they commit to following the path God has set before them — the roadblocks disappear. To borrow a line from the PBS black history series: they've got to keep their Eyes on the Prize. But be clear, friends: The prize is not something they capture; the prize is who they become.

So the Hebrews open their eyes and . . . wow! The wind shifts, the Spirit moves (not unlike what happens years later on Pentecost), and the waters are held back. Miracles happen once we make the decision to go forward. The forces in creation work *for* our good, because the good we're seeking is God's good, the freeing of our true souls. "Everything works for good with those who love God."

The Hebrews seize the "window of opportunity" just as the Allied forces did on D-Day. They cross the sea and gather on dry land on the other side. The Egyptian chariots are swallowed by the sea. It is time to give thanks to God.

There will be new roadblocks, new external ones. But the most troublesome will be the old *internal* roadblocks coming back to haunt them — fears, doubts, and low esteem that will make them consider taking their eyes off the prize. It will be a struggle, but they will not give up. They will persevere, believing God wants them to succeed.

So it is with us. Individually and corporately we must work to *uncover* or *discover* God's vision for us. Some of us must *recover* it. We must *honor* it and ask God to help us achieve it. We must seek the help of others and assist them as they pursue God's plan for them. Some of us can be the backpacker who offered to walk with the man seeking to claim his inheritance. Others must look for hikers to walk with.

Still others of us can be what I call "coin scratchers," people who find a tarnished coin in the dirt and scratch off the corrosion to see if it's a dime or a penny. People whose self-image is so tarnished they have no way of knowing the soul inside them: they need the help of us "coin-scratchers."

But even there we find a trap. We can be seduced into helping others while avoiding our own souls' callings. I'm so busy helping you become your true self I can't take time to work on my self. It may be a convenient excuse.

But freeing the angels, the true selves within, that's the primary task. We'll be pursued by self-doubts like snakes and wolves. Negative memories will claw at us and wail, "You'll fail; you can't do it. Give up trying to learn the piano; you'll never play Carnegie Hall. There's no money in piano playing." Red Seas and chasms with rickety rope bridges will appear. Images of low esteem will pursue us like armed Egyptian soldiers in chariots. Signs will announce ROAD CLOSED. The road behind will beckon, saying, "Ahh, being a slave's not so bad; being a chicken plucker's not so awful."

But we can call for help. We can call for help from the one who has placed this dream, this hope, within us. We can call on God our Creator and Sustainer. Eyes on the prize. The roadblocks will be removed. Seas will part. Hikers and angels will appear as if by magic. We must have faith. As Yoda tells Luke Skywalker in *The Empire Strikes Back*:Trust the force. God will be with us. God will be with us.

Proper 20
Pentecost 18
Ordinary Time 25
Exodus 16:2-15

Meeting Our Needs, Not Our Greeds

Once upon a time there lived a farmer who raised chickens, wonderful, plump, juicy chickens that cooked up beautifully.

But one summer a problem arose. It seemed that a fox had found a way to sneak into the pen where the chickens were kept, and it carried off a chicken every night. The farmer tried setting traps, but the fox was too smart to take the bait and get caught in the trap. The farmer tried staying awake and watching over the chicken pen, but he never did spot where it was that fox got in. No matter what the farmer tried, each morning when he checked, another chicken would be gone.

One morning he noticed one chicken was gone, but another had a mark on it, as if the fox had tried to snatch two chickens at once.

"Aha," said the farmer to himself. "This is no longer a hungry fox; it is a greedy fox." That same night the farmer took two of his plumpest chickens and laced them together — two chickens, three legs — so they looked like they were entered in a three-legged sack race at the county fair.

The next morning when the farmer awoke, he found the fox in his chicken yard, the pair of laced-together chickens blocking the tunnel that the fox used to get under the fence. Its mouth was still around the two chickens, and it refused to let go of its prize. The farmer had no trouble shooting it. The fox's greed had led to its own undoing.

There's a big difference between meeting needs and meeting greeds, isn't there?

Now I'm not saying greedy people don't ever get their greed needs met, because we've only got to look around us to see that some of them do. Not all of them get their just desserts the way the fox did. But I am prepared to say that God cares about us and will help us meet our needs. Period. God will help meet our needs, not our greeds. If we insist on meeting our greeds, we're on our own.

The Hebrews who have fled Egypt are wandering around, trying to put the past behind them, looking for a better future. There's no doubt they need help. They're hungry, thirsty, tired, homeless. So they grumble and complain (one way of making their needs known), doing it through their leader Moses. Moses prays to God, and God answers the people's prayers. They need food, so God sends flocks of quail in the evening. In the morning, at dawn, God sends "bread from heaven," a thin flaky substance that forms and is described as being like a frost. They call it manna dew.

What more could they ask for? Their prayers have been answered. Where there seemed to be no possible sustenance, God sent sustenance. What more could they ask for?

God must have known what they were like, because God gave instructions to go along with the manna. They are to gather only what they need for each day, and no more. God clearly says that any extra they try to hoard will spoil. You see, God knows their needs and their greeds.

Nevertheless, being humans, the Hebrews (some of them) don't heed the instructions. They gladly receive this gift of salvation, this unexpected sustaining manna from heaven. (It doesn't say they ate the quails. Nor were there special instructions given about them.) Their greed takes over, and some of them try to stockpile the manna — even though they've been told to take only what they need.

So the extra manna the Hebrews try to stockpile does indeed spoil, a fact that leaves them grumbling all the more. Their stomachs have been fed, but their greed hasn't.

There's more. The writer of the passage wants to make sure we know it is God's hand in this, that it's not just some phenomenon or pattern which these poor, uneducated Hebrews don't pick up on. After all, based on a week's worth of experience, they might figure the rule of thumb for manna goes something like this: Manna Spoils After One Day.

But God says they can collect *two days' worth* of this bread from heaven on the sixth day — one day's worth for the sixth day and another day's worth for the seventh or Sabbath day. That way they won't be working on the Sabbath, and they can rest, worship, and be together.

But won't that extra day's provisions spoil? No, for God allows them to collect up enough to meet their needs — not only physical needs but their spiritual needs, too, including rest on the Sabbath day. God is willing to help meet their needs, not their greeds.

College professor William Least Heat Moon lost his teaching position in Columbia, Missouri. He could have wallowed in self-pity, but instead trusted the Great Spirit (Moon's heritage is Native American) to meet his needs. He set out to see and write about this country by sticking to America's back roads, called "blue highways." *Blue Highways* became the title of the unemployed professor's book which turned out to be an unexpected best-seller. It didn't make him a fortune, but it gave him enough money that he could concentrate on what he did best — not teaching, but full-time writing. Note, however, that William Least Heat Moon wasn't out to meet his greeds. He was simply doing what he believed God or the Great Spirit called him to do and to be.

We in America are caught up in a culture that promotes greed. Our worst instincts are played to by advertisers needing to hawk their wares — from luxury cars to yachts to diamonds as big as a fist. We are wooed by six commercials per break in a television show, bombarded by promises of easy no-pain credit, and seduced by beautiful faces promising either that we can enjoy the lifestyles of the rich and famous or we can benefit from the bargains flashed at us on the Home Shopping Channel.

Not that it's wrong to want things or to have things. But we're frequently confusing wants and needs, needs and greeds. Advertising no longer communicates information to help us meet a need; now it *convinces* us we can't do without something that we don't even need. The old copywriter's maxim advised: "Sell the sizzle and not the steak." We've come to believe we can't live without the sizzle, and further, that we *deserve* the sizzle as well as the steak.

We have become shamefully greedy — pushing people out of the way for (or paying scalpers' prices for) Cabbage Patch Dolls, Pet Rocks, or whatever's the fad. We have overfished the Grand Banks and other areas, depleting the seas. We've almost made extinct rhinos for their horns and elephants and whales for their ivory. We've cut down rainforests hundreds and thousands of years old. But worse, we've come to believe the lies that come with the greed — that it's okay to be greedy. We've shut our ears to God's commands that we be good stewards of everything we've been given dominion over — the earth, the plants, the animals, and to some degree our brothers and sisters.

We are not much different from the Hebrews in today's scripture lesson. We fail to listen. Our greed clogs our ears. We want two, three, four, 100 days' worth of manna dew — all in one in-gathering.

Or put it into a framework Jesus used. We are so intent on building bigger barns that we can fill with sports cars — more, more, more — that we become too future-oriented. We miss the present. We miss out on life now, today. We fail to hear Jesus' words to the man who kept building bigger barns for his more and more crops: "You fool, this very night your soul will be required of you."

As with the hungry Hebrews and the manna dew, God will give us what we need. In those times when we need more, as with the double helping of manna to cover the weekend's two days, God will provide. But not if we want two days' worth simply to meet our greed.

There is another side to this manna story, one we must read between the lines to get. What if the people spent all their time gathering manna — days' and weeks' and months' worth of it, as much as they could collect and store up? They would have no life together. What would happen to relationships? They'd become slaves to their own greed, and is that so different from the slavery they fled in Egypt?

Perhaps a closing illustration can help. It comes from one of our better television theologians, Michael Landon.

In one episode of *Little House On The Prairie*, farming hasn't worked out, so Pa Ingalls moves the family to a new state. Gold has been discovered there, so Pa decides it's worth a try. They stop in town for provisions and meet a minister who befriends them. A conversation about Sunday school ensues. When the wagon is loaded, Pa Ingalls says (with that winning Michael Landon smile), "S'long, Reverend. Maybe you could say a prayer we find gold."

To which the wise and kindly minister says, "I can't ask God to help you locate gold, Mr. Ingalls, but I will pray for you and your family's happiness and welfare."

Pa Ingalls looks lovingly at Ma Ingalls, and you can see that the minister's words have at least momentarily gotten them back on track, helped them reorder their priorities. Pa says (again with that winning Michael Landon smile), "That'd be fine, Reverend. That'd be just fine." Off they drive.

We who watch *Little House On The Prairie* find ourselves resonating to that. We sense the danger, and we somehow know the value being lifted up in that scene: God helps meet our needs, not our greeds.

Let's put it another way. If you were Pa Ingalls and the minister said he could pray for one or the other — finding gold or for you and your family's happiness and welfare — which would you choose?

God will meet our need, not our greed. Let us give attention to God's instructions about how to use what we are given wisely. Let us be a people of thanksgiving, grateful for both the manna which feeds our bodies and the Christ, the bread from heaven, who feeds our souls. Let us harken to the Word and wisdom of our God.

Proper 21
Pentecost 19
Ordinary Time 26
Exodus 17:1-7

But You Can't Get Water Out Of A Rock!

"You can't get blood out of a turnip!" we've all heard (usually in response to a bill collector or a higher church budget). Or we've heard a variation, "You can't squeeze water out of a stone." We nod our heads in agreement with the speaker. After all, how can we argue with something so plain? The rational, analytical side of our brain says, "True, true, sad but true. You can't get water out of a rock." Oh, we of little faith. All we see is the rock.

Every week when I need to come up with a sermon, I read the prescribed scripture passage(s) for that Sunday and scratch my head. "Come on," I say. "I *need* a sermon." Nothing comes out. I stare at the page and think, "This is like squeezing water out of a rock." What I see is the rock — not the potential for water. I see the blank page, not the potential for a sermon. It's not until I trust God to reveal the sermon behind the page that it comes out. (Maybe not masterpieces, but I've never yet gotten into the pulpit Sunday morning and said, "Sorry, no word from God.")

We're all like those Hebrews at times, aren't we? They're wandering in the wilderness, thirsting to death and grumbling about it. "Moses," they say, "we and our families and our animals are dying of thirst. Help."

69

So Moses approaches God, and God tells him to go to a certain spot and to strike the rock with his staff, assuring him water will appear. Moses does as he is told and, wow, where before they'd seen only rock, water flows.

Imagine the Hebrews' reaction. Cheering, clapping, whistling, people saying "Neat-o!" and "Cool!" But they probably believed the miracle was that water appeared where there had been no water. That's not the case. It's not that there was no water there. The water was there; it's just that they couldn't *see* it there, didn't have access to it, didn't know how to tap it. The true miracle wasn't water appearing where there was no water; the true miracle was they stopped seeing rock and finally saw water beneath.

Richard Bach, in his terrific little paperback, *Illusions: The Adventures Of A Reluctant Messiah,* writes: "Argue for your limitations, and sure enough, they're yours."[1]

We must stop arguing for limitations, stop arguing "You can't get water out of a rock." We must ask God to help us see the water, the potential in our lives and in all of life's situations. Argue for your limitations, and sure enough, there they are, limiting you.

A minister tells this story. "When I decided to enter seminary, my wife and I didn't have two cents. We had piles of bills. Seminary would mean no income for me, little income for her, and the paying out of grad school tuition on top of rent, food, and household expenses. The thought terrified me. All I could see was the rock.

"In the spring of that year my wife, her parents, and I traveled to Maine for my entrance interview at Bangor Theological Seminary. My in-laws had a small camper, so we stayed in a campground outside Bangor. The interview went well, but my concern wasn't that I wouldn't get accepted — my concern was that I would, for I had no idea how the bills would be met. But I trusted God would help us through.

"The day we were to return home, my father-in-law went out to unhook the electric cables and sewer hose. He came back inside and said, 'The man in the next camper asked if you'd join him and his wife for a prayer.' I was annoyed at my father-in-law for telling the man I was becoming a minister.

"The couple was from California and simply wanted to give me a copy of a book they liked, an old Christian classic, *Streams In The Desert*. (I hadn't thought about the significance of the title until now.) The man asked me to pray aloud, something I was uncomfortable doing, but I did it. He thanked me and I left. I never saw them again.

"On our way home I opened the book to read what the man had written on the flyleaf. Not only had he inscribed the flyleaf of the book, but he had inscribed a check for $100 to the seminary and me. A total stranger. Suddenly I began to see the water, not just the rock."[2]

Piero Ferrucci says in his book, *Inevitable Grace*: "How often — even before we began — have we declared a task 'impossible'? And how often have we construed a picture of ourselves as being inadequate? ... A great deal depends upon the thought patterns we choose and on the persistence with which we affirm them."[3] We must let God help us see the water, not just the rock.

A Vermont Methodist church declined in the 1960s and '70s. It boasted 800 members on the rolls in 1963, but by 1982 the number at Sunday worship was 28-30. Attached to the back of the church was a two-story structure with a basement. It had overflowed with children and youth in the 1960s, but in 1982 sat empty, no Sunday school at all. The thermostat was set low to keep expenses down. Except for worship, that church had no signs of life. The attached building was termed "our albatross." Parishioners spoke of it as a liability, something that cost them money.

A new pastor arrived in 1983 and remarked, "An empty building. Great. How shall we use this ... *asset*?"

A couple of weeks went by and a used hospital bed was advertised in the newspaper, free for the taking. The pastor arranged to pick it up and stored it in the basement of the albatross building. The church bulletin noted the bed was available on free loan to anyone needing it. In no time, a woman recovering from hip surgery called.

But a week later someone else needed it. When the pastor mentioned the dilemma during worship, a woman stood and said she had another hospital bed in her attic and she'd donate it. Soon word got out about what came to be known as the Hospital Equipment Loan Program. Canes, crutches, walkers, shower seats, and wheelchairs were donated. The cellar of the albatross building — canes and crutches hanging everywhere — looked like the Healing Shrine at Lourdes. A volunteer church secretary came to work in the church office 3 mornings a week — not to type the church bulletin, but to keep the in/out log for hospital equipment!

The program was so successful the church started a Second Hand Clothing Shop on the main floor. A special-needs pre-school program moved in. An ecumenical Soup Kitchen project took hold. The vision changed — from seeing the old Educational Building as an albatross, a liability, to seeing it as an Outreach Ministries Building, an asset. The church stopped seeing the rock and trusted God to let the water flow. Today they average close to 150 at worship and are brimming with exciting programs.

Seeing the water applies to churches, but also to our personal lives. Somerset Maugham wrote: "It's a funny thing about life; if you refuse to accept anything but the best, you very often get it."[4]

We mustn't listen to that little voice that insists on holding us back, advises us we don't deserve the abundance God has for us. That Censor, that Pessimist, will always whisper, "But the rock, the rock," instead of "The water, the water."

I'll close with an old tale some of you know, "Stone Soup," but with a slightly different spin.

The war was over, and a soldier trudged toward home. He approached a town as another soldier was leaving it.

"Have you anything to eat?" the first soldier asked.

"Not a thing," said the second. "And the townfolk have nothing. The war has hit them hard, so don't waste your time. You can't get water out of a stone." The two parted company, and the first soldier walked toward the town.

Ka-flooey. He tripped and fell. When he looked to see what he'd stumbled on, there in the road lay a round stone. He didn't know what he might do with it, but he fancied the stone, so he tucked it into his knapsack.

In town he waved to people, but no one waved back. Wherever he asked for food, people offered excuses instead. "Poor harvest." "Not enough for my own family." "Sorry, got to keep some for seed." "Too many mouths to feed. Can't spare it."

Finally the hungry soldier stopped under a tree in the town square. He prayed he might at least *dream* a delicious meal. He lay his head on his knapsack, the stone making a hard pillow, and fell asleep. He dreamed of a wonderful soup, with people laughing, dancing, enjoying it together.

The soldier awoke and called the town together, announcing that if someone would bring forth a cauldron of water, he would make the specialty he was known far and wide for — Stone Soup. Despite many odd looks and much skepticism, someone got the kettle of water. When the pot boiled, the soldier took the stone from his backpack, raised it over his head, prayed, and plunked it in the water.

A few minutes later he tasted it. "My, this is delicious, the best Stone Soup I've ever made. Now if only I had a couple of cabbages, it'd give it a much richer flavor." A woman ran home and returned with two cabbages which the soldier cut up and put into the cauldron.

A while later he tasted it again. "A couple of carrots and some milk and this would be fit for a nobleman." A farmer sent his son home to fetch carrots and milk. When he came back with them, into the soup they went.

And so it went. Each time the soldier tasted the soup, he mentioned an ingredient — salt, pepper, onions, beef — and the ingredient would appear. The aroma of the Stone Soup soon had everyone's mouth watering.

Finally the time came to serve it. The townspeople set up tables and chairs. Wine and bread appeared on the tables. Fiddlers played. Everyone danced and ate the delicious Stone Soup together. The town came alive as it hadn't in years, and laughter rang out like church bells.

When the time came to leave, the soldier presented the stone to the townspeople, suggesting they use it once a month the way they had just done. He waved and got back onto the main road.

Before long he ran into the soldier he'd met earlier. The other soldier said, "See? A waste of time, right? Didn't I tell you? You can't get water out of a stone."

To which the first soldier simply smiled and said, "Water? You expect too little, my friend. Not only water from a stone, but great soup and warm fellowship."

Will we, individually and as a people of God, see the rock and not the water? The liabilities and not the assets? Will we continue to listen to the voice that says, "You can't get water out of a rock ... or soup from a stone?"

We must trust God, who says through the lips of Jesus, "I have come that you may have life, and have it more abundantly." We must trust God, who shows us through Moses that which seemed before unimaginable — that water can indeed spring from a rock. The water is there. The water is there already. We just need to ask God to help us to see it.

---

1. Richard Bach, *Illusions: The Adventures Of A Reluctant Messiah* (New York: Dell, 1977), p. 100.

2. Steve Burt, in a sermon preached September 4, 1994, at the United Church of Stonington, Connecticut.

3. Piero Ferrucci, *Inevitable Grace* (Los Angeles: Jeremy P. Tarcher, 1990).

4. Found in Julia Cameron, *The Artist's Way* (New York: Putnam's, 1992), p. 177.

Lectionary Preaching
After Pentecost

The following index will aid the user of this book in matching the correct Sunday with the appropriate text during Pentecost. All texts in this book are from the series for Lesson One, Revised Common Lectionary. Lutheran and Roman Catholic designations indicate days comparable to Sundays on which Revised Common Lectionary Propers are used.

(Fixed dates do not pertain to Lutheran Lectionary)

Fixed Date Lectionaries *Revised Common and Roman Catholic*	Lutheran Lectionary *Lutheran*
The Day of Pentecost	The Day of Pentecost
The Holy Trinity	The Holy Trinity
May 29-June 4 — Proper 4, Ordinary Time 9	Pentecost 2
June 5-11 — Proper 5, Ordinary Time 10	Pentecost 3
June 12-18 — Proper 6, Ordinary Time 11	Pentecost 4
June 19-25 — Proper 7, Ordinary Time 12	Pentecost 5
June 26-July 2 — Proper 8, Ordinary Time 13	Pentecost 6
July 3-9 — Proper 9, Ordinary Time 14	Pentecost 7
July 10-16 — Proper 10, Ordinary Time 15	Pentecost 8
July 17-23 — Proper 11, Ordinary Time 16	Pentecost 9
July 24-30 — Proper 12, Ordinary Time 17	Pentecost 10
July 31-Aug. 6 — Proper 13, Ordinary Time 18	Pentecost 11
Aug. 7-13 — Proper 14, Ordinary Time 19	Pentecost 12
Aug. 14-20 — Proper 15, Ordinary Time 20	Pentecost 13
Aug. 21-27 — Proper 16, Ordinary Time 21	Pentecost 14
Aug. 28-Sept. 3 — Proper 17, Ordinary Time 22	Pentecost 15
Sept. 4-10 — Proper 18, Ordinary Time 23	Pentecost 16
Sept. 11-17 — Proper 19, Ordinary Time 24	Pentecost 17

Sept. 18-24 — Proper 20, Ordinary Time 25	Pentecost 18
Sept. 25-Oct. 1 — Proper 21, Ordinary Time 26	Pentecost 19
Oct. 2-8 — Proper 22, Ordinary Time 27	Pentecost 20
Oct. 9-15 — Proper 23, Ordinary Time 28	Pentecost 21
Oct. 16-22 — Proper 24, Ordinary Time 29	Pentecost 22
Oct. 23-29 — Proper 25, Ordinary Time 30	Pentecost 23
Oct. 30-Nov. 5 — Proper 26, Ordinary Time 31	Pentecost 24
Nov. 6-12 — Proper 27, Ordinary Time 32	Pentecost 25
Nov. 13-19 — Proper 28, Ordinary Time 33	Pentecost 26 Pentecost 27
Nov. 20-26 — Christ the King	Christ the King

Reformation Day (or last Sunday in October) is October 31 (Revised Common, Lutheran)

All Saints' Day (or first Sunday in November) is November 1 (Revised Common, Lutheran, Roman Catholic)